One beautiful morning
    A dad said to his son
Let's go on an adventure
    I'm sure we'll have fun.

Good Eye Little Spy

Published by
@TheQuillsTip
Cedar Rapids, Iowa
ISBN # 978-0-9837999-3-1

Copyright 2019 by @TheQuillsTip.
All Rights Reserved.

Illustrated by CyAn Platas.

For more information about this book, please contact us:
contact@hartmannfamily.us

Written by @TheQuillsTip

The road led to the city
 Where there'd surely be
Some very old buildings
 For them to see.

The dad drove onto the highway
   Where lots of cars drove past.
Here there were one and two and three lanes
   So the cars can drive fast.

As they drove along the highway
   The son said to his dad,

"Look at that old truck,
   He looks grumpy and mad!"

Later, the dad took an exit,
For he wanted to go

Far from the highway,
Where he could drive nice and slow.

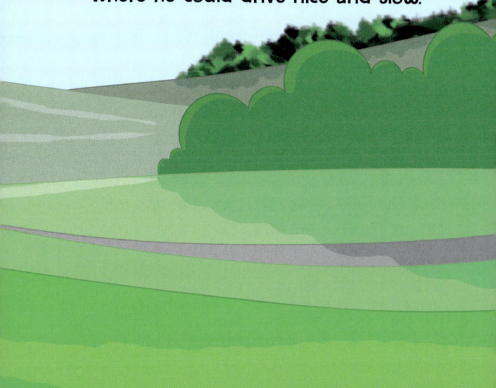

As they drove along the windy road,
The son said to his dad,
"See all those silly goats,
All the billies, mommies, dads?"

As they drove on and on,
　　　The road came to a town
Where no one was smiling
　　　They all wore a frown.

As they drove on through,
    The son said to his dad,

"I wish people smiled here;
    This makes me feel bad."

"Good eye little spy,"
    Said the dad to his son,
"Where are the smiles at;
    Why are there none?"

"Good eye little spy,"
       Said the dad to his son.
"We're back home now,
       And I hope you had fun."

The End.

Made in the USA
Lexington, KY
28 November 2019

Sunsets
AND GRANITE COUNTER TOPS

CARL STARS

FriesenPress

Suite 300 - 990 Fort St
Victoria, BC, V8V 3K2
Canada

www.friesenpress.com

Copyright © 2021 by Carl Stars
First Edition — 2021

All rights reserved.

No part of this publication may be reproduced in any form, or by any means, electronic or mechanical, including photocopying, recording, or any information browsing, storage, or retrieval system, without permission in writing from FriesenPress.

ISBN
978-1-03-911003-8 (Hardcover)
978-1-03-911002-1 (Paperback)
978-1-03-911004-5 (eBook)

1. BIOGRAPHY & AUTOBIOGRAPHY, PERSONAL MEMOIRS

Distributed to the trade by The Ingram Book Company